In His Presence

DISCOVERY SERIES BIBLE STUDY
For individuals or groups

"**H**ow's your prayer life?" the well-meaning father asked his son. The bright, church-going 14-year-old shrugged his shoulders, "I don't really pray that much."

"Why not?" the concerned father pressed.

"I don't really need anything."

That honest teenager put words to what many of us are afraid to admit out loud—we don't pray unless we need something.

In the following pages, staff writer Dennis Fisher takes a look at our common struggle to make time for God. Along the way, he gives us some practical pointers that will help us as we strive to pray, read God's Word, and serve others in the process.

This Discovery Series Bible Study is based on
In His Presence: Spending Time Wtih God (QO718), one of the popular Discovery Series
booklets from Our Daily Bread Ministries. Find out more about Discovery Series at
discoveryseries.org

Discovery House is affiliated with Our Daily Bread Ministries,
Grand Rapids, Michigan.

Requests for permission to quote from this book should be directed to:
Permissions Department, Discovery House, PO Box 3566, Grand Rapids, MI 49501, or contact
us by e-mail at permissionsdept@dhp.org

Discovery House.®
from Our Daily Bread Ministries

Managing Editor: Dave Branon
Study Guide questions: Sim Kay Tee
Graphic Design: Steve Gier

COVER PHOTO:
Fred Fokkelman via FreeImages.com

INSIDE PHOTOS:
Partheeban Moorthy via Pixabay.com, p.6; Glenn Eaton via RGBStock.com, p.10; Alvimann via MorgueFile.com, p.12;
Frank Meitzke via Pixabay.com, p.13; Jorge Guillen via Pixabay.com, p.18; Bryan Dowdey via Pixabay.com, p.20;
Bonnyb Bendix via Pixabay.com, p.21; Annazuc via Pixabay.com, p.26; PublicDomainPictures via Pixabay.com, p.28;
Marja Flick-Buijs via RGBStock.com, p.29; Mconnors via MorgueFile.com, p.34; Sue Anna Joe via FreeImages.com, p.36;
Chelle via MorgueFile.com, p.37; Penywise via MorgueFile.com, p.44; Darren Hester via FreeImages.com, p.46

ISBN: 978-1-62707-336-3
Printed in the United States of America
First Printing in 2015

Table of Contents

How To Use

DISCOVERY SERIES BIBLE STUDIES

The Purpose

The Discovery Series Bible Study (DSBS) series provides assistance to pastors and lay leaders in guiding and teaching fellow Christians with lessons adapted from Discovery Series booklets produced by Our Daily Bread Ministries and supplemented with items taken from the pages of *Our Daily Bread*. The DSBS series uses the inductive study method to help Christians understand the Bible more clearly.

The Format

READ: Each DSBS book is divided into a series of lessons. For each lesson, you will read a few pages that will give you insight into one aspect of the overall study. Included in some studies will be FOCAL POINT and TIME OUT FOR THEOLOGY segments to help you think through the material. These can be used as discussion starters for group sessions.

RESPOND: At the end of the reading is a two-page STUDY GUIDE to help participants respond to and reflect on the subject. If you are the leader of a group study, ask each member to preview the STUDY GUIDE before the group gets together. Don't feel that you have to work your way through each question in the STUDY GUIDE; let the interest level of the participants dictate the flow of the discussion. The questions are designed for either group or individual study. Here are the parts of that guide:

MEMORY VERSE: A short Scripture passage that focuses your thinking on the biblical truth at hand and can be used for memorization. You might suggest memorization as a part of each meeting.

WARMING UP: A general interest question that can foster discussion (group) or contemplation (individual).

THINKING THROUGH: Questions that will help a group or a student interact with the reading. These questions help drive home the critical concepts of the book.

DIGGING IN: An inductive study of a related passage of Scripture, reminding the group or the student of the importance of Scripture as the final authority.

GOING FURTHER: A two-part wrap-up of the response: REFER suggests ways to compare the ideas of the lesson with teachings in other parts of the Bible. REFLECT challenges the group or the learner to apply the teaching in real life.

OUR DAILY BREAD: After each STUDY GUIDE session will be an *Our Daily Bread* article that relates to the topic. You can use this for further reflection or for an introduction to a time of prayer.

Go to the Leader's and User's Guide on page 47 for further suggestions about using this Discovery Series Bible Study.

The Starting Point

As we begin to think together about the struggle to make time for God in our lives, it's essential that we establish a purpose for considering this topic.

The practice of spending time praying and reading the Bible is not our ultimate goal in this life. And the act of seeking opportunities for moments with God can be rather empty—if we do not understand the most important purpose God has for us on this earth.

Before we examine how to spend time with God, it is important first that we are certain that we know Him.

Centuries ago, a religious leader named Nicodemus approached Jesus to find answers to his own spiritual questions. Nicodemus said, "We know that you are a teacher who has come from God. For no one could perform the signs you are doing if God were not with him" (JOHN 3:2).

Jesus' response seems surprisingly unrelated to Nicodemus' comments: "Jesus replied, 'Very truly I tell you, no one can see the kingdom of God unless they are born again' " (v. 3).

Their conversation underscored the contrast between physical life and spiritual life. In the garden of Eden, before Adam disobeyed God, he was in a state of complete innocence. But after Adam disobeyed God by eating the forbidden fruit, a fundamental change took place. A great barrier to fellowship between God and man damaged their relationship. Adam realized this, and he hid from God (GENESIS 3:8–10).

Sin had created an insurmountable chasm where once there had been an intimate union between God and man. That same alienation affects each of us today. Here's how the Bible describes it: "We all, like sheep, have gone astray, each of us has turned to our own way" (ISAIAH 53:6).

The tragic result of this rebellion against God is spiritual death.

We cannot have any kind of fellowship with God—the subject of this booklet—until that changes.

That's why Jesus' words to Nicodemus in John 3 are such good news! Jesus told him that each of us can be made alive again on the inside. God's Holy Spirit can come inside us and restore our fellowship with God.

The Lord is eager to forgive our sin, restore a relationship with God, and give us the gift of eternal life.

> You may think of yourself as a Christian because you attend church or grew up in a family that worshiped together. It is of eternal importance that you know for sure.

But how does that happen?

First, we must admit that we are sinners and that we cannot save ourselves. In Romans 3:23, we read this: "All have sinned and fall short of the glory of God."

Next, we must recognize that our sinfulness has serious consequences. Later in Romans we read, "The wages of sin is death" (6:23).

> "The wages of sin is death, but the gift of God is eternal life in Christ Jesus our Lord."
>
> ROMANS 6:23

But here is the good news—the best news. Christ took our punishment for our sins when He died on the cross. Here's how Paul, who wrote the book of Romans, explains it: "God demonstrates his own love for us in this: While we were still sinners, Christ died for us" (5:8). Jesus, the perfect One, gave up His own life as our substitute. He died for us. He rose from the dead to prove His power over death, and He still lives today in heaven as our Savior.

Here's where we come in. John 1:12 says, "to all who did receive him [Jesus], to those who believed in his name, he gave the right to become children of God."

If we recognize our sinful condition and then put our faith and trust in Jesus to forgive us our sins through His death, burial, and resurrection, we receive the gift of eternal life and the pleasure of fellowship with God right now.

When that happens in our lives, we will want to get to know God better through reading His Word, the Bible. We will want to talk to Him in prayer.

> "God made him who had no sin to be sin for us, so that in him we might become the righteousness of God."
>
> 2 CORINTHIANS 5:21

And we will want to feel the closeness of true fellowship with Him.

So, if you have trusted Jesus as Savior and long to spend valuable, encouraging, and uplifting time with the Lord, read on. Enter His presence and spend time with the God of the universe, the master Creator, and the author of your salvation.

The Starting Point

STUDY GUIDE
read pages 6–9

1

To know how to have a personal relationship with God.

MEMORY VERSE
John 1:12—

"Yet to all who did receive him, to those who believed in his name, he gave the right to become children of God."

Warming Up

Who is your best friend? How did you and he or she become such good friends?

Thinking Through

1. Why do you think the author says that "The practice of spending time praying and reading the Bible is not our ultimate goal in this life" (page 6)? What then is our ultimate goal in this life?

2. Why would it be meaningless for you to spend time with a stranger or one who with whom you would not want to develop a personal relationship?

3. Why is spending time with a loved one so important?

Going Further

Refer
What does John 1:12 say about your relationship with God?

1. What does it mean to be "born again" (v. 3)?

2. Jesus says that "everyone who believes may have eternal life" (v. 15). What does it mean for you to have "eternal life"?

3. What do verses 16–17 tell you about how you can have a personal relationship with God?

[1] Nicodemus . . . . [2] came to Jesus at night and said, "Rabbi, we know that you are a teacher who has come from God. For no one could perform the signs you are doing if God were not with him."

[3] Jesus replied, "Very truly I tell you, no one can see the kingdom of God unless they are born again."

[4] "How can someone be born when they are old?" Nicodemus asked. "Surely they cannot enter a second time into their mother's womb to be born!"

[5] Jesus answered, "Very truly I tell you, no one can enter the kingdom of God unless they are born of water and the Spirit."

[14] "Just as Moses lifted up the snake in the wilderness, so the Son of Man must be lifted up, [15] that everyone who believes may have eternal life."

[16] For God so loved the world that he gave his one and only Son, that whoever believes in him shall not perish but have eternal life. [17] For God did not send his Son into the world to condemn the world, but to save the world through him. [18] Whoever believes in him is not condemned, but whoever does not believe stands condemned already.

Prayer Time ➤

Use the *Our Daily Bread* article on the next page as a guide for reflection on spending quality time with God.

Reflect

How do you become a child of God? Why is it necessary for you to "receive Jesus" and "believe in Jesus" to have a relationship with God?

If you have a personal relationship with God, why would it be important for you to spend time with God?

Check the Oil

When I helped our daughters learn to drive, I included a little instruction on basic auto maintenance. We visited a local service station where the girls learned to check the oil every time they put fuel in the car. Today, years later, they often remind me of my six-word slogan, "Oil is cheap; engines are expensive." Adding a quart of oil is nothing compared to replacing an engine.

Maintenance is also important in our spiritual lives. Taking time each day to read the Bible, pray, and listen to God is a key element in avoiding a breakdown. In Psalm 5, David wrote, "My voice You shall hear in the morning, O LORD; in the morning I will direct it to You" (v. 3 NKJV). In the verses that follow, he poured out his heart in praise, thanksgiving, and requests to God.

Many people find it essential to begin every day with the Lord. Before checking email, catching the news, or eating breakfast, they find some quiet moments alone to read a portion of God's Word, praise Him for His greatness, thank Him for His love, and seek His guidance. Others spend time reading and praying at different times of the day.

It's not magic—it's maintenance, as we ask the Lord each day to fill our hearts with His presence on the road of life.

—*David McCasland*

PSALM 5:3—

My voice You shall hear in the morning, O LORD; in the morning I will direct it to You (NKJV).

■ Read today's *Our Daily Bread* at **odb.org**

The Fellowship Problem

Right after creation of the first man and woman, the Bible tells us, God was "walking in the garden in the cool of the day" (GENESIS 3:8). The Creator of the universe did not hide from His creatures behind closed doors or angelic assistants. Instead, He sought out Adam and Eve for spiritual companionship.

The same fellowship-seeking God who walked with Adam and Eve in the cool of the day is reaching out to each of us today.

This is what a quiet time is all about—spending time with God to experience His presence, comfort, and guidance.

Many of us wish to have a meaningful quiet time with God, yet we find

■ FOCAL POINT

A quiet time is a special time set aside for conversation with God. This often includes prayer, Scripture reading, and meditation. It is often daily and done at a specific time.

ourselves in an environment where that is difficult. This may lead to a sense of guilt if we neglect our personal devotional time with God. But if we measure our spirituality by counting the number of times we have met with God during the week, we have missed the point. Devotions are a matter of our heart, not just an appointment on our calendar.

As a sophomore in college, I had a discipline problem. All kinds of activities and distractions competed with getting assignments in on time and preparing for exams. The busyness of life constantly caused me to replace one activity with another or to neglect some things entirely. Not only did I not seem to get things done but I was also having a hard time making a plan for getting things done.

One night after class, I discussed my problem with a professor. He recommended that I prioritize my daily schedule. As I considered his advice, I felt compelled to single out time with God as the top priority of each day. That would be one "to do" that always got done, regardless of whatever else might fill my day. Planning it for the first thing in the morning would help ensure I got it done.

But the next day, as I began my new commitment my resolve sagged. Time with God seemed like too much effort in exchange for too little reward. I simply wasn't in the mood.

I admitted my feelings to the Lord. I told Him my heart was cold, and I felt little motivation to spend time with Him. I confessed my apathy and thanked Him for His forgiveness.

Then I chose to give my mood to God. I asked Him to replace my stagnation and apathy with His vitality. Rereading my devotional passage for the day, I prayed for real transformation. As I began to pray over the projects that needed my attention later in the day, I told God about my assignments and asked Him for the strength necessary to do my best with them.

By the time my feet hit the asphalt on the way to class, I had begun to feel an energy, a focus, and—most important—a discipline I had previously lacked. That semester my grades went up. God had answered my prayer. As I continued to ask God to solidify my new commitment to spend time with Him, I found the strength I needed.

The prophet Isaiah wrote, "Those who wait on the LORD shall renew their strength" (ISAIAH 40:31 NKJV). The prophet's promise to the people of ancient Israel still holds true for us today. The Hebrew word for *renew* means "to substitute, to exchange, to show newness, to sprout." But the kind of waiting that renews strength is active, not passive. It is a deliberate exchange of human effort for divine strength. We are not expected to dig deep and tap into an unknown reserve of our own willpower and determination. Instead, we are to ask God to give us His energy—we ask Him to supply our strength.

 # Our Model

As we seek to spend time with God, who better to look at as our example than Jesus? During His life on earth, Jesus limited the exercise of His divine powers. Although fully God, He depended on the Father and the indwelling Holy Spirit working through Him. That dependence was demonstrated by the way Jesus

---

■ FOCAL POINT

Times when Jesus retreated to pray:
- Matthew 26:36ff.
- Mark 1:35; 6:46; 14:32-39
- Luke 5:16; 6:12; 9:18; 11:1; 22:41ff.
- John 18:1

sought time alone with His Father. The Gospels record multiple times when Jesus left the crowds and His followers behind for solitary communion with the Father.

Mark 1:32–39 records one such occurrence. A closer look at the text shows the importance and impact of our Lord's own devotional life and what we can learn from it. "Very early in the morning, while it was still dark, Jesus got up, left the house and went off to a solitary place, where he prayed" (1:35).

After a long evening of healing sick and demon-possessed people (1:29–34), Jesus actively made time to commune with God. I believe Christ used this time to regain His spiritual center.

> One such "alone with God time" was
> during Jesus' prayer in the Garden of
> Gethsemane just before His crucifixion.
> "My father, if it is not possible
> for this cup to be taken away unless I drink it,
> may your will be done."
> MATTHEW 26:42

 ## Our Distractions and God's Directions

"Simon and his companions went to look for him, and when they found him, they exclaimed: 'Everyone is looking for you!' Jesus replied, 'Let us go somewhere else— to the nearby villages—so I can preach there also. That is why I have come' " (MARK 1:36–38).

The word *found* in verse 37 could be translated "hunted down." Thinking they knew best how Jesus could spend His day, Peter and his friends sought Him out. They were willing to interrupt the Lord's prayer time with their own urgent concerns: "Everyone is looking for you!"

But Jesus didn't worry about being perceived as unresponsive or uncaring. Did His quiet time make Him less sensitive to the people near Him? Just the opposite. It seems that as a result of His time alone with the Father, Jesus desired to continue with His larger mission: "to seek and to save the lost" (LUKE 19:10). Meeting only the needs of those directly in front of Him would have been to ignore God's concern for all who are lost. Jesus' resolve was solidified after His time with the Father.

Jesus used His time alone with God for meaningful fellowship as well as for strength and direction to carry on with His mission. If we desire the same results from our time alone with God, we need to follow Jesus' example and apply God's Word in the power of the Spirit—not just letting it influence what we do but letting it change the very people we are.

If time alone with God is seen as a once-a-day spiritual oasis or as merely something to be checked off on our "to do" list, we may fall into the trap of separating our spiritual life from the rest of our life. That's a subtle mistake we need to avoid. Time with God is our spiritual lifeline. From the garden of Eden until now, God has desired to walk with His people in every part of life's journey.

The Fellowship Problem

To know the importance of spending time with God daily.

"Very early in the morning, while it was still dark, Jesus got up, left the house and went off to a solitary place, where he prayed."

Warming Up

If you are stranded on an island with only one person, who is that one person you would love to spend more time with? Why?

Thinking Through

1. If you are to talk with a non-Christian about "quiet time," how would you explain what quiet time is, what is its purpose, and why quiet time is important for Christians?

2. Do you find it difficult to maintain a consistent quiet time? Why or why not? What hinders you from spending time with God?

3. What does the author mean when he says, "Devotions are a matter of our heart, not just an appointment on our calendar" (page 14)? Why would you agree or disagree?

Going Further

Refer

Read Isaiah 40:31 in the New King James Version. What does it mean for you to "wait on the LORD"? Why is it important for you to "wait on the LORD"?

1. What kind of schedule did Jesus have (vv. 32–34, 37)? What are some of the pressures Jesus might have faced?

2. Why do you think Jesus needed to pray (v. 35)? And why at such an early hour and in such a solitary place?

3. What does Jesus' example teach us about time management and about doing what is truly important, not what is urgent?

32 That evening after sunset the people brought to Jesus all the sick and demon-possessed. 33 The whole town gathered at the door, 34 and Jesus healed many who had various diseases. He also drove out many demons, but he would not let the demons speak because they knew who he was.

35 Very early in the morning, while it was still dark, Jesus got up, left the house and went off to a solitary place, where he prayed. 36 Simon and his companions went to look for him, 37 and when they found him, they exclaimed: "Everyone is looking for you!"

38 Jesus replied, "Let us go somewhere else—to the nearby villages—so I can preach there also. That is why I have come." 39 So he traveled throughout Galilee, preaching in their synagogues and driving out demons.

Prayer Time ➤

Use the *Our Daily Bread* article on the next page as a guide for reflection on spending quality time with God.

Reflect

1. Do you consider spending time with God a non-negotiable part of your daily schedule? Why or why not? What are some distractions that hinder you from keeping this quiet time consistently?

2. Dennis Fisher said, "I believe Christ used this time to regain His spiritual center" (page 16). What does "regaining one's spiritual center" mean? What is important that you also "regain your spiritual center"?

Getting Beyond Us

I have one of those friends who seems to be better than I am at just about everything. He is smarter; he thinks more deeply; and he knows where to find better books to read. He is even a better golfer. Spending time with him challenges me to become a better, more thoughtful person. His standard of excellence spurs me on to greater things.

That highlights a spiritual principle: It's crucial for us to spend time in God's Word so we can connect with the person of Christ. Reading about the impact of Jesus' unconditional love for us compels me to love without demand. His mercy and His free distribution of grace to the most undeserving make me ashamed of my tendency to withhold forgiveness and seek revenge.

I find myself becoming a more thankful person when I realize that, despite my shameful fallenness, the Lord has clothed me in the beauty of His perfect righteousness. His amazing ways and unsurpassed wisdom motivate and transform me. It's hard to be content with my life as it is when in His presence I am drawn to become more like Him.

The apostle Paul calls us to the joy of beholding Christ. As we do so, we are "transformed into the same image from glory to glory" (2 CORINTHIANS 3:18 NKJV).

—*Joe Stowell*

2 CORINTHIANS 3:18—

We all,… beholding as in a mirror the glory of the Lord, are being transformed (NKJV).

■ Read today's *Our Daily Bread* at **odb.org**

3

The Intentional Preparation

People who love each other are intentional about spending meaningful time together. To do this, discipline and love must work together. Finding time requires deliberate planning.

A similar intentionality is necessary to cultivate meaningful time with God. We see this deliberate relational approach modeled by Jesus: He set aside time alone and allowed that time to have an impact on Him. Often we begin the day intent on having devotions at a set time, but as the day goes on, one item after another bombards and distracts us until devotions are postponed or forgotten until the next day.

But when we center ourselves in God, things fall into perspective, and a quiet time becomes a priority rather than something we squeeze into our leftover time.

This relational connection requires discipline.

In 1 Corinthians 9, the apostle Paul used the imagery of athletic games to illustrate the need for spiritual discipline. The term translated *strict training* (v. 25) literally means "the power of self-control; to practice abstinence."

When athletes commit to the Olympics, they avoid anything that might distract them. Disciplined exercise and rigorous diet are essential. Similarly, by setting up a daily devotional discipline and, through God's strength, making it a priority, the results can amaze us.

Here are some ways to set up a quiet time:

Set realistic expectations. I knew a student who was an excellent writer. The problem was that he consistently turned in his papers late. "If I can't do it right, I won't do it," he declared. His commitment to perfectionism caused him to do things that actually damaged his grade rather than improve it.

Many of us have a similar approach to maintaining a quiet time. We often decide to "throw the baby out with the bathwater." If we cannot do it exactly the way we want, we don't do it at all."

■ FOCAL POINT

"Therefore I do not run like someone running aimlessly; I do not fight like a boxer beating the air. No, I strike a blow to my body and make it my slave so that after I have preached to others, I myself will not be disqualified for the prize."   1 CORINTHIANS 9:26–27

Perfectionism

Perfectionism and tyranny of the urgent can be enemies of our quiet time with God. Some time with God is better than no time with God.

But devotional time with God is not about perfection; it is about progress. It is better to have a short and deliberate time than to skip it entirely in the name of high standards. Perfect circumstances rarely occur, and if we wait to have devotions until they do, we may never have them.

Find the right place. In his book *Letters to Malcolm*, C. S. Lewis has a surprising suggestion regarding devotional times. His advice is to make sure there is "just the right amount of distraction" to help us concentrate. Lewis tells of a man who had his devotional time in a railroad compartment because complete silence left too much temptation for his mind to wander. The sounds of the railcar forced him to concentrate. His focus was enhanced when it was slightly challenged.

> "Devotional time with God is not about perfection; it is about progress."

The point is that we're not always going to find a place that is as quiet as an undiscovered cave. We need to find the place that best fits our needs and enhances our quiet time.

Reserve a daily time. Many people emphasize the importance of starting the day with devotions. I once heard someone say that the code for his own devotional life was, "No Bible, no breakfast." This commitment may have worked for him, but devotions may be better for you at midday or even late at night. That will depend on your metabolism, occupation, or lifestyle. Everyone is different.

The Bible encourages meeting with God at any time of the day. David wrote, "O God, You are my God; early will I seek You" (PSALM 63:1 NKJV). He also mentioned his anticipation to meditate on God's Word during the "watches of the night" (PSALM 119:148). Daniel prayed at three set times a day (DANIEL 6:10). And the first psalm refers to the blessed man whose "delight is in the law of the LORD, and who meditates on his law day and night" (1:2).

There is wonderful freedom about meeting times with God. It is up to us to decide what time of day is best suited for us to meet with Him. What matters most is the commitment to having a daily time when God can speak with you through His Word and you can respond to Him in prayer.

> "There is wonderful freedom about meeting times with God. It is up to us to decide what time of the day is best suited for us to meet with Him."

Whether we need a highly disciplined schedule or prefer a more relaxed one, we all need a plan. Use a wall calendar, smart phone, daily planner, computer, or any other type of calendar to mark the daily time set aside to meet with God.

It's better to be brief and consistent. A music instructor said, "It's better to practice fifteen minutes a day every day than to practice several hours just two days a week."

This principle easily applies to our devotional time. It is better to block out just fifteen minutes and to consistently keep that time than to let our

Fixed Prayer Times

Many Christian traditions practice fixed hour prayers—morning, mid-day, and evening praying is a way to grow in and discipline your prayer life.

daily discipline be eaten away by multiple distractions and then try to make up with one or two long sessions with God. Manageable devotional times, even if they are brief, get us in the practice and may lead to more consistent and longer times. After prayerfully deciding how much time to spend, write it on your calendar.

3

STUDY GUIDE
read pages 21–25

To learn how to set up a consistent quiet time to spend with God daily.

MEMORY VERSE
Psalm 42:2—

"My soul thirsts for God, for the living God. When can I go and meet with God?"

Warming Up

Do you agree or disagree that spending time with God is not a priority for a lot of Christians? Why or why not?

Thinking Through

1. How would you agree or disagree with the author when he says, "devotional time with God is not about perfection, it is about progress" (page 23)?

2. Do you think C. S. Lewis' advice to have your quiet time at a place where there is "just the right amount of distraction" (page 23) is a good suggestion? Why or why not? Where do you usually have your quiet time? Why there?

3. Do you agree or disagree that a "No Bible, no breakfast" (page 23) code is the best way to have your quiet time? Why or why not? What better alternative code would you suggest?

Going Further

Refer

Read Psalm 63:1–8. How do the metaphors "thirst" (v. 1) and "soul . . . satisfied with marrow and fatness" (v. 5) speak of David's earnest yearning for God (v. 1)? What blessings await him as he spends time with God (vv. 2–8)?

1. What do the metaphors of a runner competing in a race (v. 24) and a boxer fighting in the ring (v. 26) say about the Christian life?

> 24 Do you not know that in a race all the runners run, but only one gets the prize? Run in such a way as to get the prize. 25 Everyone who competes in the games goes into strict training. They do it to get a crown that will not last, but we do it to get a crown that will last forever. 26 Therefore I do not run like someone running aimlessly; I do not fight like a boxer beating the air. 27 No, I strike a blow to my body and make it my slave so that after I have preached to others, I myself will not be disqualified for the prize.

2. Are you competing in a sprint event or a marathon? Why would this be important? In terms of your Christian life, what would constitute "strict training" for you (v. 25)?

3. What prize are you hoping to win (vv. 24, 27)? What would disqualify you for the prize (v. 27)?

Prayer Time ➤

Use the *Our Daily Bread* article on the next page as a guide for reflection on spending quality time with God.

Reflect

1. "Earnestly I seek you; I thirst for you, my whole being longs for you" (PSALM 63:1). To what extent do David's words express your own earnest desire to want to spend time with God?

2. Review the steps for setting up a quiet time with God in this chapter. Which of these four steps do you find yourself struggling with? If so, what needs to be changed so you can have a more consistent quiet time?

Times of Refreshing

What do you find most refreshing? A cold drink on a hot day? An afternoon nap? Listening to praise and worship music?

The biblical theme of refreshing has a variety of physical and spiritual meanings. In Scripture we read of refreshment by resting on the Sabbath (EXODUS 23:12), with cool water after physical activity (JUDGES 15:18–19), by soothing music (1 SAMUEL 16:23), and with encouraging fellowship (2 TIMOTHY 1:16).

The apostle Peter describes a time of spiritual refreshment that took place on the Day of Pentecost. He exhorted his listeners to repent and respond to the gospel "that times of refreshing may come from the presence of the Lord" (ACTS 3:19 NKJV). The apostle's statement was especially meaningful to the Jewish audience with its reference to the millennium when Messiah would rule. But the good news of spiritual life would also be extended to the Gentiles (ACTS 10).

Even now as believers we can experience a time of refreshing by quieting our hearts in a devotional time of prayer and Bible reading. When we spend time alone with the Lord, we can experience His peace and joy, which renew us in spirit. Aren't you thankful for these daily times of spiritual refreshment?

—*Dennis Fisher*

ACTS 3:19—
Repent..., so that times of refreshing may come from the presence of the Lord (NKJV).

■ Read today's *Our Daily Bread* at **odb.org**

4

The Functional Practice

Discipline is not the only thing necessary in our devotional times. Relationships are built through communication, and two-way communication is better communication.

God speaks to us. In time past, God spoke directly to His people. In 1 Samuel 3:21, we read that God "revealed himself to Samuel through his word."

The Hebrew word for *reveal* means to "show or uncover." The Creator disclosed His thoughts, character, and will to His servant. Today, God's communication comes mainly through the Bible, and the Holy Spirit enlightens our minds as we read it.

In approaching a portion of Scripture, the following time-honored process, with the aid of the Holy Spirit, can help make examining the Word of God fruitful.

First we must ask: **"What does the passage say?"** We answer this by looking at the message of the passage in its original context. Allow the Bible passage to speak for itself in its original historical and cultural setting.

Second we ask: **"What does it mean?"** Meaning is not limited to the original audience. Within the Bible passage is a core spiritual truth that is meaningful in all ages. We should strive to discover the message a passage has for us today.

Finally we ask: **"How does it apply?"** The Holy Spirit can change our thoughts, speech, and behavior when we allow Him to use the principle we find in God's Word to shape us. Another way to phrase the question is this: "In what ways should my life change as a result of studying this passage?"

We respond to God. Have you ever written a letter in which you opened the depths of your heart? How would you feel if you received a response to that letter that ignored everything you wrote and talked only about issues that concerned the other person?

The Bible is a love letter from our heavenly Father. It is the story of the depth of His love for us. Yet often our communication with God is one-sided; we read His message to us and respond with prayers that are about us. Instead of responding to the love letter, we ignore its content and focus solely on our own pressing needs.

As we pray, we are free to tell God all of the things that concern us. But remember, you have just heard from Him through His Word about what concerns Him. Take the time to respond to what you have read. Thank Him for His promises. Rejoice in the instruction we have received. Confess where the Holy Spirit is convicting. Revel in the insight into His character. Ask him for deeper, clearer understanding of what a passage means and what it means as we strive to be transformed more like Christ.

Daniel 6:10 says of Daniel: "Three times a day he got down on his knees and prayed, giving thanks to his God." As Daniel made his requests known to God, a spirit of thanksgiving permeated his prayer times, despite his difficult circumstances. Our prayers should be marked by a similar sound of thanksgiving for who God is and what He has done for us.

> We should ask, "How does this portion of Scripture apply? In what ways should my life change as a result of studying this passage?"

Writing it down. Keeping a written record of what we discover in our quiet time will reveal trends in our journey of faith. We will see progress in various areas of our life that may go unnoticed were they not written down.

The devotional guide on page 32 could be copied in a notebook and kept as a record of daily quiet times.

DEVOTIONAL GUIDE

Date:_____

PASSAGE: _____

INSIGHTS: _____
_____
_____
_____
_____
_____
_____
_____
_____
_____
_____
_____
_____
_____
_____
_____
_____

APPLICATION: _____
_____
_____
_____

PRAYER: _____
_____
_____
_____
_____

The practice of writing things down helps us remember what we have learned and keeps it fresh in our minds so we can continue to be affected and challenged by it for the rest of the day.

Jesus was perfect, yet He looked for undistracted time with God. Why? Because He functioned on earth as all humans are meant to function—in total obedience on the Father. His life on earth was spent in perfect submission to His Father. We gained insights from Jesus' own "quiet time" in the previous pages. We can also learn from Jesus how to allow our times with God to make a difference for us throughout the day.

The Functional Practice

To know that God reveals himself to us through the Bible.

Warming Up

Why is two-way communication so important if we want to build relationships? What might happen to a relationship without two-way communication?

Thinking Through

1. Why did the author say that "the Bible is a love letter from our heavenly Father" (page 30)?

2. What does the author mean when he warns that "often our communication with God is one-sided" (page 30)? Why would you agree or disagree? How can you make it into a two-communication?

3. In addition to telling God our concerns and needs, what else ought we be talking through with God in our prayers?

Going Further

Refer

What do 2 Timothy 3:15–17 and Hebrews 4:12 teach about the importance of God's Word in our lives?

1. What did the psalmist say about God and His Word (vv. 89–104)?

2. What blessings await those who trust in and obey God's Word (vv. 89–104)?

3. How does the psalmist show that he loved God's Word (v. 97)?

89 Your word, LORD, is eternal; it stands firm in the heavens. 90 Your faithfulness continues through all generations; you established the earth, and it endures.

91 Your laws endure to this day, for all things serve you. 92 If your law had not been my delight, I would have perished in my affliction.

93 I will never forget your precepts, for by them you have preserved my life. 94 Save me, for I am yours; I have sought out your precepts. 95 The wicked are waiting to destroy me, but I will ponder your statutes. 96 To all perfection I see a limit, but your commands are boundless.

97 Oh, how I love your law! I meditate on it all day long. 98 Your commands are always with me and make me wiser than my enemies. 99 I have more insight than all my teachers, for I meditate on your statutes. 100 I have more understanding than the elders, for I obey your precepts. 101 I have kept my feet from every evil path so that I might obey your word. 102 I have not departed from your laws, for you yourself have taught me.

103 How sweet are your words to my taste, sweeter than honey to my mouth! 104 I gain understanding from your precepts; therefore I hate every wrong path.

Prayer Time ≫

Use the *Our Daily Bread* article on the next page as a guide for reflection on spending quality time with God.

Reflect
1. Share one thing you have learned about who God is in your quiet time this week.

2. Thank God for that "one thing" He has done for you this past week.

Reflections

Not long ago, I passed a milestone marking 20 years since I began keeping a spiritual journal. As I reread my first few entries, I was amazed I ever kept it up. But now you couldn't pay me to stop!

Here are some benefits I have received from journaling: From life experiences, I see that progress and failure are both part of the journey. I'm reminded of God's grace when I read how He helped me to find a solution to a major problem. I gain insight from past struggles that help with issues I am currently facing. And, most important, journaling shows me how God has been faithfully working in my life.

Many of the psalms are like a spiritual journal. They often record how God has helped in times of testing. In Psalm 40, David writes: "I waited patiently for the LORD; and He inclined to me, and heard my cry. He also brought me up out of a horrible pit, out of the miry clay, and set my feet upon a rock, and established my steps" (vv.1–2 NKJV). Later, David needed only to read that psalm to be reminded of God's faithful deliverance.

Journaling may be useful to you too. It can help you see more clearly what God is teaching you on life's journey and cause you to reflect on God's faithfulness.

—Dennis Fisher

PSALM 40:2—
He also brought me up out of a horrible pit . . . and set my feet upon a solid rock (NKJV).

■ Read today's
Our Daily Bread at
odb.org

5

The Ultimate Payoff

Have you ever felt that your quiet time didn't do you much good as you went out to face the day? That the time and effort you put into spending time in God's Word and in prayer had no impact on your problems? That your devotional time didn't really have any importance for the rest of your day, as though the two really had nothing to do with each other? This is called *compartmentalization*—confirming your spiritual life to an exclusive part of the day. But God never intended for us to live this way. He is eager to walk with us, helping us through life's struggles.

Jesus' encounter with the two disciples walking on the road to Emmaus, recorded in Luke 24:13–31, contains insights for us about conversing with God throughout the day.

> *Now that same day two of them were going to a village called Emmaus, about seven miles from Jerusalem. They were talking with each other about everything that had happened. As they talked and discussed these things with each other, Jesus himself came up and walked along with them; but they were kept from recognizing him* (LUKE 24:13–16).

Little is known outside of this account about the two who walked the path from Jerusalem to Emmaus, but the Bible indicates that they were troubled. They had an internal conflict—an emotional struggle over a disappointing experience—and they were discussing it.

It was in the middle of their sorrow and confusion that Jesus approached them as they walked. "Jesus himself came up and walked along with them" (v. 15). How wonderful! The risen Christ joined them on their

> "Be strong and courageous. Do not be afraid or terrified because of them, for the LORD your God goes with you; he will never leave you nor forsake you."
>
> DEUTERONOMY 31:6

journey. He wants to join us as well. Life is a journey and Christ wants to be our constant companion as we walk our own dusty trails. He desires more from us than a conversation at the occasional rest stop.

Acknowledge the road bumps. One of life's greatest challenges is trying to make sense of the apparent contradictions and setbacks we face. Much of our confusion comes from the fact that we are limited in our perspective;

we only have part of the picture. The two people on the road to Emmaus were caught in the middle of this very problem. Not only did they not understand many of the things that had happened but also the events that had unfolded were contrary to what they had expected. Jesus saw their struggle and helped them address it.

> He asked them, "What are you discussing together as you walk along?" They stood still, their faces downcast. One of them, named Cleopas, asked him, "Are you the only one visiting Jerusalem who does not know the things that have happened there in these days?" "What things?" he asked. "About Jesus of Nazareth," they replied. "He was a prophet, powerful in word and deed before God and all the people. The chief priests and our rulers handed him over to be sentenced to death, and they crucified him; but we had hoped that he was the one who was going to redeem Israel. And what is more, it is the third day since all this took place. In addition, some of our women amazed us. They went to the tomb early this morning but didn't find his body. They came and told us that they had seen a vision of angels, who said he was alive. Then some of our companions went to the tomb and found it just as the women had said, but they did not see Jesus" (vv. 17–24).

Responding to Christ's question, the two detailed what was troubling them. Their summary was a concise review of the hope they held that Jesus of Nazareth was the Messiah who would redeem the nation of Israel. Instead, He had been crucified. Their hopes and the hopes of many others died with Him on the cross. As if their minds were not already reeling, they had heard reports that His tomb was now empty, and several of their friends had received visits and heard messages from angels.

The two, who had walked with the Lord only days before, had soar-

> One of life's greatest challenges is trying to make sense of the apparent contradictions and setbacks we face.

ing hopes. Now their dreams were shattered. They viewed life—and especially the recent events—through a keyhole. That is what it means to be human. Humans are finite and can take in only part of the picture of any circumstance. These two took what they thought they knew and measured it against what they had experienced, and things didn't add up. Our experience is just like theirs.

Often, what we believe doesn't make sense from our limited perspective. Whether it's our disappointed expectations of how God should answer a prayer or how we view life's apparent misfortunes, we must remember that we are limited in our understanding.

But Jesus wants us to tell Him our concerns. He is ready to provide a listening ear as we tell Him about the details, great and small, of our lives. The believer's unique relationship with Christ allows prayerful communication in the middle of any circumstance.

> Often, what we believe doesn't make sense from our limited perspective. We must remember that we are limited in our understanding.

Let Jesus explain. It must have been devastating for Jesus' followers to have their hopes and dreams crushed with such seeming finality. But when Christ used the light of the Scriptures to illuminate their experience, they began to get a fresh outlook on their circumstances.

> *He said to them, "How foolish you are, and how slow of heart to believe all that the prophets have spoken! Did not the Messiah have to suffer these things and then enter his glory?" And beginning with Moses and all the Prophets, he explained to them what was said in all the Scriptures concerning himself* (vv. 25–27).

Jesus' response sounds abrupt: "How foolish you are!" The original Greek wording translated *foolish* literally means "without knowledge." The two disciples on the road didn't know the full story.

Jesus provided the only solution to the problem—additional information. The Teacher explained to them, from key passages in the Scriptures, why the events of the last few days should not have been surprising. He enlightened them about how the Messiah must suffer before being glorified.

The lesson for us is that though we struggle with disappointment, we too lack the knowledge that puts everything in perspective and allows us to understand. The Lord may eventually provide the necessary information to help us make sense of our circumstances. But sometimes we won't get an answer before the coming of Christ in His eternal kingdom. Remaining teachable, sometimes despite our circumstances, and being in regular contact with our Teacher gives our faith and knowledge opportunity to grow.

Await divine activity. Meaningful connection with the risen Christ makes us want to linger with Him. When the two on the road reached their destination, they felt a strong need to stay close to the Savior.

> *As they approached the village to which they were going, Jesus continued on as if he were going farther. But they urged him strongly, "Stay with us, for it is nearly evening; the day is almost over." So he went in to stay with them* (vv. 28–29).

The disciples had heard what this stranger had to say for several miles, but they wanted to hear more. "Stay with us," they insisted.

He joined the two for their evening meal, and the presence of the divine opened the possibility for the supernatural. Including the Lord in the routine affairs of our daily life opens the door for His work in every area of life.

> *When he was at the table with them, he took bread, gave thanks, broke it and began to give it to them. Then their eyes were opened and they recognized him, and he disappeared from their sight. They asked each other, "Were not our hearts burning within us while he talked with us on the road and opened the Scriptures to us?"* (vv. 30–32).

After Jesus shared and blessed the bread, the disciples' eyes were opened and they recognized Him. Earlier, "they were kept from recognizing him" (v. 16). But now they saw the stranger's new identity.

Likely in shock at the sudden revelation and subsequent disappearance of the Lord, the two reflected on what it was like to be walking with Jesus and having Him teach them the Scriptures. Their hearts burned as the Scriptures were explained with divine insight and authority. The same Greek word used for their eyes being "opened" (v. 31) is used to explain how Jesus "opened" the Scriptures to them (v. 32). He penetrated their minds with understanding.

> The disciples' hearts burned as the Scriptures were explained with divine insight and authority.

Recognizing Christ in the Scriptures and in our experiences should occur throughout the day rather than being limited to a once-a-day event.

Building a relationship is not easy. It requires diligence, discipline, communication, patience, trust, and time. A relationship with God is no exception. The preceding pages were written to give hope, inspiration, and a plan for moving forward with God. Spend time with Him in His Word and in prayer. Take your conversation with Him into every part of your daily life. Allow Him to speak to you and take time, often, to speak with Him. As you do, your life with God will develop and deepen. As it does, you will find that the results are well worth the effort.

5 The Ultimate Payoff

read pages 37–43

MEMORY VERSE
Luke 24:32—

"Were not our hearts burning within us while he talked with us on the road and opened the Scriptures to us?"

To know the value of lingering with Jesus and meditating on Scriptures when going through life's difficult circumstances.

Warming Up

Do you sometimes feel that it is a waste of time to do your quiet time?

Thinking Through

1. What is *compartmentalization* and the bad outcomes of this (page 37)? How do you overcome compartmentalization in your life?

2. How have the trials and troubles, suffering and pain in your life affected your quiet time with God?

3. Why do you think life's painful circumstances tend to draw you away from God? What steps can you take to ensure that these painful experiences draw you nearer to God, instead of away from Him?

Going Further

Refer

Read Luke 24:28–35. Why do you think "as they approached the village to which they were going, Jesus continued on as if he were going farther" (v. 28)? What does this passage (vv. 29–31) teach you about the value of spending sufficient time with Jesus and lingering with Him?

1. What major setbacks did the two disciples experience? If you were Cleopas (v. 18), how would you recount what has happened so far (vv. 14, 17–24)?

2. If you were helping the two disciples, what would you do to encourage them? How did Jesus help these two disciples overcome their sense of helplessness and disappointment?

3. Why do you think Jesus did a Bible study with the two disciples instead of performing a miracle to encourage these distraught disciples? What was the focus of the Bible study, and why is this important (vv. 25–27)?

13 Two [disciples] were going to a village called Emmaus, about seven miles from Jerusalem. 14 They were talking with each other about everything that had happened. 15 . . . Jesus himself came up and walked along with them; 16 but they were kept from recognizing him.

17 He asked them, "What are you discussing together as you walk along? . . . 18 Cleopas asked him, "Are you the only one visiting Jerusalem who does not know the things that have happened there?"

19 "What things?" he asked.

"About Jesus of Nazareth," they replied...." 20 The chief priests and our rulers handed him over to be sentenced to death, and they crucified him;... 22 Some of our women amazed us. They went to the tomb early this morning 23 but didn't find his body. They came and told us that they had seen a vision of angels, who said he was alive. 24 Then some of our companions went to the tomb and found it just as the women had said, but they did not see Jesus."

25 He said to them, "How foolish you are, and how slow to believe all that the prophets have spoken! 26 Did not the Messiah have to suffer these things and then enter his glory?" 27 And beginning with Moses and all the Prophets, he explained to them what was said in all the Scriptures concerning himself.

Prayer Time ▶

Use the *Our Daily Bread* article on the next page as a guide for reflection on spending quality time with God.

Reflect

Reflect on "Life is a journey and Christ wants to be our constant companions as we walk our own dusty trails. He desires more from us than a conversation at the occasional rest stop" (page 38). What "dusty trail" are you walking at this moment?

How will spending time talking with Jesus and meditating on the Scriptures help you walk the dusty road?

Stay Connected

I woke up one morning and discovered that my Internet connection was not working. My service provider conducted some tests and concluded that my modem needed to be replaced, but the earliest they could do so was the next day. I panicked a little when I thought about being without the Internet connection for 24 hours! I thought, *How am I going to survive without it?*

Then I asked myself, *Would I also panic if my connection with God was disrupted for a day?* We keep our connection with God alive by spending time in His Word and in prayer. Then we are to be "doers of the Word" (JAMES 1:22–24 NKJV).

The writer of Psalm 119 recognized the importance of a connection to God. He asked God to teach him His statutes and give him understanding of His law (vv. 33–34). Then he prayed that he would observe it with his whole heart (v. 34), walk in the path of God's commandments (v. 35), and turn away his eyes from looking at worthless things (v. 37). By meditating on God's Word and then applying it, the psalmist stayed "connected" to God.

God has given us His Word as a lamp to our feet and a light to our path to lead us to Him.

—*C. P. Hia*

Psalm
119:105—
Your word is a
lamp for my
feet, a light on
my path.

■ Read today's
Our Daily Bread at
odb.org

■ LEADER'S and USER'S GUIDE

Overview of Lessons: In His Presence

Pulpit Sermon Series (for pastors and church leaders)

Although the Discovery Series Bible Study is primarily for personal and group study, pastors may want to use this material as the foundation for a series of messages on this important issue. The suggested topics and their corresponding texts from the Overview of Lessons above can be used as an outline for a sermon series.

DSBS User's Guide (for individuals and small groups)

Individuals—Personal Study

- Read the designated pages of the book.
- Carefully consider the study questions, and write out answers for each.

Small Groups—Bible-Study Discussion

- To maximize the value of the time spent together, each member should do the lesson work prior to the group meeting.
- Recommended discussion time: 45 minutes.
- Engage the group in a discussion of the questions—seeking full participation from each member.

Note To The Reader

The publisher invites you to share your
response to the message of this book
by writing Discovery House,
P.O. Box 3566, Grand Rapids, MI 49501,
USA. For information about other
Discovery House books, music, videos,
or DVDs, contact us at the same address
or call 1–800–653–8333. Find us on the
Internet at **dhp.org** or send e-mail to
books@dhp.org.